THRONE ROOM

USHERED *into the*
PRESENCE *of* GOD

THRONE ROOM

USHERED *into the*
PRESENCE *of* GOD

CECE WINANS

with CLAIRE CLONINGER

INTEGRITY®
PUBLISHERS
Nashville

THRONE ROOM

Copyright © 2004 by CeCe Winans.

Published by Integrity Publishers, a division of Integrity Media, Inc.,
5250 Virginia Way, Suite 110, Brentwood, TN 37027.

HELPING PEOPLE WORLDWIDE EXPERIENCE *the* MANIFEST PRESENCE *of* GOD.

Published in association with CW Entertainment.

Unless otherwise indicated, Scripture quotations are taken from The Holy Bible, New
International Version (NIV), copyright © 1973, 1978, 1984, International Bible Society. Used by
permission of Zondervan Bible Publishers.

Other Scripture references are from the following versions:

The King James Version of the Bible (KJV).

The New King James Version (NKJV), copyright © 1979, 1980, 1982, Thomas Nelson, Inc.,
Publishers. Used by permission.

New American Standard Bible, Updated Edition (NASU), copyright © 1960, 1962, 1963, 1971,
1972, 1973, 1975, 1977, 1995 by the Lockman Foundation. Used by permission.

Cover Design: The Office of Bill Chiaravalle | www.officeofbc.com
Interior Design: Susan Browne Design, Nashville, TN

Winans, CeCe.
  Throne room : ushered into the presence of God / by CeCe Winans.
    p. cm.
  ISBN 1-59145-147-7 (hardcover)
  1. Worship. I. Title.
  BV10.3.W56 2004
  248.3—dc22
                            2003024795

Printed in the United States of America
04 05 06 07 08 RRD 9 8 7 6 5 4 3 2 1

CONTENTS

SECTION ONE:
WELCOME TO THE WONDER OF WORSHIP

1

SECTION TWO:
SONGS ON THE *THRONE ROOM* CD

87

SECTION THREE:
QUESTIONS FOR REFLECTION

131

SECTION
ONE

WELCOME TO THE WONDER OF WORSHIP

Jesus, my awesome Lord and Savior

I want your name to be the first Word in this book

Just like you are the first Love in my life

The first Song on my lips

The first and only Hope in my heart.

Lord, I ask you to lead everyone who reads these pages

To see you as you are—

So beautiful, so powerful, so worthy of our worship.

I pray all of these things in your precious, holy Name,

Amen.

CONTAGIOUS JOY

The greatest joy in my life is worshiping the Lord! As you read my thoughts and ideas about worship and share some of the experiences I've had as a worshiper, I pray that my enthusiasm for worship will be contagious. I pray that in some way I can usher you into a more joyful and meaningful place as a worshiper. If that happens, then this book will have hit its mark.

THE BLESSING OF TRUE WORSHIP

In my ministry I find myself singing and praying with many different Christians from many different parts of the body of Christ. And God has begun to show me that there are some wonderful, believing Christians who pray and sing but who don't seem to enter fully into worship. I know that they love the Lord, and I know that their hearts are tender toward him. But it seems that some of these precious brothers and sisters are missing out on what it is to worship at a deep level.

Actually, I don't think it is hard to miss true worship if we have never been led there. If we've never been led to let go of our own thoughts and shut down our distractions and focus our heart and mind totally on the Lord, will we find that place of worship in this busy, noisy world? If we've never been led to enter into his presence with reverence and awe, will we ever come worshipfully before the One who is holy and

> **IF WE'VE NEVER BEEN LED TO SHUT DOWN OUR DISTRACTIONS AND FOCUS OUR HEART AND MIND TOTALLY ON THE LORD, WILL WE FIND THAT PLACE OF WORSHIP IN THIS BUSY, NOISY WORLD?**

worthy of our worship? If we've never been encouraged to open our heart and surrender ourselves completely to the God who longs to hear our voice lifted to him in worship, will we ever find our way to the Throne Room?

And here is the most important question of all: Suppose we never find that place where we can fully and freely enjoy the presence of the Lord in worship—what difference would it make? What would it matter?

It's not that we wouldn't go to heaven. It's not that God would love us less. It's that we would be missing one of the most awesome and powerful blessings that the Father has to give to his children: the blessing of true worship.

Worship can act as a weapon of warfare or as an instrument of peace. It can build faith, kindle joy, transform lives, and inspire hope. Worship can heal our heart, comfort our sorrows, and draw us closer to the Lord. And the most important gift of all is that worship allows us to see the Lord as he is, in all of his awesomeness.

I believe the Father is holding out this incredible gift of worship to each of us right now, saying, "Come, my child. Here's a taste of heaven that I want you to have every day while you're on earth." Now why would any of us turn our back on that? Why wouldn't we want to take advantage of that blessing?

The Bible says in John 4:23 that "a time is coming and has now come when the true worshipers will worship the Father in spirit and truth, for they are the kind of worshipers the Father seeks." You see, the Lord is seeking worshipers. He's seeking all of us to go deeper with him in worship. So if you feel there may be a deeper place of worship you could enjoy, I believe that's because he's tugging at your heart. That's the reason I'm writing this book.

> I BELIEVE THE FATHER IS HOLDING OUT THIS INCREDIBLE GIFT OF WORSHIP TO EACH OF US, SAYING, "COME, MY CHILD. HERE'S A TASTE OF HEAVEN THAT I WANT YOU TO HAVE EVERY DAY WHILE YOU'RE ON EARTH."

THE JOY OF THE FATHER'S WELCOME

Do I see myself as an expert on worship? No. I see myself as a child of God who has been drawn into the arms of a loving Father. I see myself as someone who was once lost but has now been welcomed into the presence of an awesome Savior and filled with the power of an amazing Holy Spirit. I see myself as the daughter of a mighty King, a daughter who has been called to meet with her Father in his Throne Room. Does that make me an expert? Well, if it does, then you must be an expert, too.

Because he's calling you to meet him in the very same place. He's longing for that special time with you. Will you come with me? Will you let me take you to the place beyond the veil? If you love him then you belong there, too. In the Throne Room, worshiping your King and mine. Your Father and mine.

I've asked the Lord to give me the words that will encourage you and lead you to that place of worship where you can enjoy his presence and he can enjoy yours. This is why he created each of us. This is our reason for being. This is the awesome purpose for our life. And the sooner we get plugged into it, the sooner we'll know the joy of our Father's welcome to the Throne Room.

CHAPTER ONE

THE LORD'S LEADING

PREGNANT WITH A PURPOSE

This book actually began with my latest project, *Throne Room*. As I chose the sixteen songs for that project, I could feel the Lord leading me to encourage the members of his body to worship. To make his Throne Room a part of their day, every day. The Lord seemed to be opening my eyes to the fact that the times we're living in have created an urgent situation. He was showing me that this is a time when we need to worship in order to combat the evil all around us. He was so definite about it that I knew what direction the CD would have to take. I almost felt like I was pregnant with a purpose and he was calling it forth.

What was being birthed in me was a worship experience—not just one or two worship songs here and there, but a complete section of uninterrupted worship that would encourage people to sing directly to the Lord. I know how powerful that can be to God's people and how our Father longs for our love and adoration.

TAKING WORSHIP TO THE CHURCHES

As I have gone to different churches to share the mission the Lord has given me, it's been wonderful. I've talked about worship, and I've shared the worship songs from the *Throne Room* project.

All of the churches have been a little bit different, but the Lord has definitely showed up in his own unique way at every place I've gone! It's been so encouraging to feel the Holy Spirit move through huge groups of people as we worshiped together.

In doing the music, I have tried to make it very, very simple so that the focus would not be on some particular song or arrangement or on my voice. I wanted to make sure that the focus was on Jesus and being with him. Sometimes we can be so fickle without even realizing it. We can wait for a certain singer or instrumentalist or worship leader. But we should always be there simply to worship the Lord and for no other reason. I wanted to make absolutely no room for entertainment in these times of worship.

It was almost as if each group I met with had its own personality. In some places, the worshipers would be crying out, "Holy, holy, holy," telling the Lord what he meant to them, and telling him in their own words how great he was. As they would draw closer to him, they would just forget about each other and forget about me. And then they would be lost in the Lord's presence. It's hard to describe how beautiful that was!

> **SOMETIMES WE CAN BE SO FICKLE WITHOUT EVEN REALIZING IT, WAITING FOR A CERTAIN SINGER OR INSTRUMENTALIST OR WORSHIP LEADER. BUT WE SHOULD ALWAYS BE THERE SIMPLY TO WORSHIP THE LORD.**

I remember one church in Tulsa. It was awesome. I could have just packed up and left town, and I think they would have all stayed there loving the Lord, they were so into worshiping him! And the thought came to me, *Wow! This is the Throne Room! This is what's going on here!*

And in some other churches the evening would be quieter and the people would be more reserved. But that was precious, too. Because when it was over, several people would come up to me, one or two at a time, and they would say, "Thank you, CeCe. I don't think I really understood worship before tonight." Or, "I didn't know how to worship, but now I do."

That was when I would feel so grateful to be where God wanted me to be—in the center of his will—and so much joy would fill my heart.

CHAPTER TWO

SUCH AN AMAZING THING

No Greater Joy

No wonder I was excited when people began telling me that for the first time they understood what worship was. Worship is such an amazing thing when you stop to think about it. It's all about being welcomed into an intimate relationship with the God who made us and loves us and desires to spend time with us.

Worship is a simple thing on one hand. It's not complicated. We don't have to take classes in it or get any special degrees. Children can worship. Old people can worship. Everyone is invited and included. It's elementary. But, on the other hand, it's mind-blowing! To think that the God who created the entire universe finds no greater joy in his huge, eternal, loving heart than hanging out with us, his children! Every time

I dwell on that for a little while, every time I let it sink in, I realize all over again what an awesome privilege true worship really is.

Two Keys: Surrender and Love

I've been a worshiper most of my life, but there's a depth in the way I worship now that I didn't always have. I think the key to deepening in the worship life is surrender. The sooner we learn to surrender, the sooner we become what God wants us to be. And that's when we find that deep place of worship.

The best news of all about worship is that God makes himself so available, so easy to get to. It's not hard at all. We human beings try to make everything so complicated. But God's not like that. He's the one who says, "Come to me . . . and I will give you rest" (Matthew 11:28). He's got such wonderful, sweet, beautiful things for us if we can just learn to let go. If we can just learn to surrender and love him.

We try to make obedience such a hard thing. We try to make it something we have to frown about and grind our teeth over and make a fist at. But Jesus doesn't make it that way. He starts by touching us with love. He says, "If you love me, you will obey what I command" (John 14:15).

He puts love first. And once we love him, obedience becomes the most natural thing in the world to do. That's why when we love him, we can worship our way right into his kingdom.

> **THE SOONER WE LEARN TO SURRENDER, THE SOONER WE BECOME WHAT GOD WANTS US TO BE. AND THAT'S WHEN WE FIND THAT DEEP PLACE OF WORSHIP.**

Surrender and love are the keys to everything. Once we surrender to him, we love him; and when we love him, worship will begin to flow out of us, and then we will long to obey him naturally.

WORSHIP AS A LOVE AFFAIR

In the Bible, the love of Christ for the church is compared to a husband's love for his wife. That helps us understand that at its most basic level, worship is like a love affair. Isn't that beautiful? That's why we need to learn to express our love for the Lord with complete freedom. We need to learn to sing our own songs to him, our own unique melodies. And we can only do this when we know him intimately, when we're comfortable in his presence. Then our songs will flow forth.

Some people say to me, "It's fine for you to say that your songs will flow forth, CeCe, because you're a singer. But I'm not a singer. I have a lousy singing voice."

Don't ever insult your Creator in that way! I promise you, whoever you are, your voice is beautiful to the God who made you! He designed you. He knows the sound of your voice very well, and it pleases him to no end. All he asks of you is to "make a joyful noise" (Psalm 100:1 KJV). You don't have to sound like a professional singer. All you have to sound like is you.

Why do you think the Lord went to so much trouble making each of us unique? Why do you think that there's not another person in the entire world exactly like you? In fact, each one of your fingerprints is entirely unique. God loves the uniqueness of you. He's crazy about you exactly as you are!

Do your friends say you have a funny laugh? He designed that funny laugh. He loves his handiwork. So don't try to be like anyone else. He's already got a CeCe. I've got the market cornered on being me. So don't desire a voice like mine. When you worship, bring God your own voice. That's the sound he's waiting to hear. That's the sound that will make him smile and bring him joy when he meets with you in worship. He loves you exactly the way he made you.

In Spirit and in Truth

When the Bible says in John 4:23 that God wants us to worship him "in spirit and truth," have you ever wondered what that means? I believe that

> **If you are feeding on the Word of God**
> **every day, if you are**
> **nourishing yourself on his truth,**
> **then those are the words you'll be**
> **giving back to God when you worship.**

worshiping in "spirit" means to worship the Lord simply and purely from your heart. And worshiping in "truth" means to worship him with words from his Word. Have you ever heard the saying "You are what you eat"? God's Word is pure truth. If you are feeding on the Word of God every day, if you are nourishing yourself on his truth, then those are the words you'll be giving back to God when you worship. The more you read his Word and feed on it—the more you chew on it and swallow it—the more it will come out of you when you open your mouth to sing or talk or worship. You won't be able to help it. Truth will be what you've fed yourself on, and truth will be what comes out of your mouth when you lift up your voice to worship God. Then you'll be worshiping in spirit and truth, and God will be pleased.

The Difference between Praise and Worship

Is there any difference between praise and worship? Some people may not make a distinction, but I see praise as acknowledging God for all the good in our life. It is declaring his greatness and his glory. Everybody has a right to praise him. We can praise him simply because he woke us up this morning, for instance. We can praise him because he put air in our lungs and provided something for us to eat today.

People praise God for all kinds of things in all kinds of circumstances. Christians praise him for his power, for his faithfulness, and for his mercy in their lives. Even people who don't really know him as their personal Lord will say things like, "Well, praise the Lord—look at that rain. I've been hoping it would rain." So praise can be very intense or pretty casual. It can come from people who love the Lord and from some who don't even know him.

Praise is wonderful. But worship moves us deeper and closer to the heart of God. It's a more intimate thing. Worship is that level of prayer, that intimate expression of love, that rises from the hearts of believers who know their Lord and know without a doubt that they'll be welcomed when they come into his presence. The Bible says in Hebrews 4:16 that we can "approach the throne of grace with confidence, so that we may receive mercy and find grace to help us in our time of need."

We don't have to tiptoe up to our God, wondering if he'll accept us. In fact, it's the Lord himself who pulls back the veil and invites us to come closer. He is the one who went all the way to the Cross for us. Now it's by his blood that we can approach him with confidence, knowing that his arms are always open to us. Ephesians 1:6 says we are "accepted in the Beloved" (NKJV). We are welcomed beyond the veil.

Worship is not about us. It's not about what we think or feel. It's not even about the Lord's ability to help us or the times he's helped us in the past. Worship is simply about our great and awesome God and who he is. Worship is being drawn to the incredible beauty and power of his love, and adoring him.

> WE DON'T HAVE TO TIPTOE UP TO OUR GOD,
> WONDERING IF HE'LL ACCEPT US. IN FACT,
> IT'S THE LORD HIMSELF WHO PULLS BACK THE
> VEIL AND INVITES US TO COME CLOSER.

WHY DO SOME PEOPLE SETTLE FOR LESS?

If it's true that Jesus is always very near and very available to us every day, why do some people seem to settle for a lukewarm prayer life? Why do some seem to love the Lord from far away instead of allowing him to draw them near to him the way he longs to? Why do so many of his followers refuse to invest the time it takes to focus on his lordship or surrender to his love? Why do so few slow down for even the short time it takes to meditate on his goodness? Why do so many settle for praise without moving into the intimacy of worship? To me that seems like settling for marriage without ever making love.

We live in a country, in a culture, in an age that rushes and hurries. We drive our cars through traffic. We take our children to school. We drive them to practice for different sports and activities. We want to be good parents. We've got to make a living. God is on our side in all of these things. He understands. But if these things mean that we're leaving him out of our life or putting him in last place, he sees us missing out on the most important thing—the thing that should be our number-one priority. And this is bound to break his heart.

PRAY FOR MORE SPIRITUAL INTIMACY

We need to pray that the Lord will show us ways to bring more intimacy with him into our spiritual life. If it means waking up fifteen or thirty minutes or an hour earlier in the morning. If it means worshiping in the car whenever we're alone. If it means taking our lunch to work and going off alone with the Lord instead of having lunch with a friend. He'll show us ways to add that spiritual intimacy we need so desperately.

Think of those older saints you know who raised huge families with no help and still managed to have amazingly close walks with the Lord. How did they do it? They were desperate for God. They threw themselves on his mercy, and he met them where they were. He gave them peace in the middle of tremendous trials, and he can do the same for us.

We need to be desperate for God, thirsty for him, just like those older saints were. Jesus is coming back soon. I truly believe that. And I'm afraid that many of us, even those of us in the church, will not be ready for him. Many of us will not know him when we see him face to face if we don't begin to know him now in worship.

CHAPTER THREE

LIVING THE WORSHIP LIFESTYLE—NOW!

THE SECRET PLACE

When you were a child, did you ever have a secret clubhouse, a hiding place, or maybe a tree house where you could meet your best friend and the two of you could share your childhood secrets? The Lord our God is the best friend we will ever have, and he is inviting us to meet him in his secret place. It's a place in the Spirit where we can approach him as worshipers, a place where we can know him in an intimate relationship. In that secret place the enemy cannot penetrate the peace that God will give us. The enemy fights hard to keep us out of God's secret place, because he realizes that once we are there, he can't disturb our peace. That's why we must learn to find that place and learn to stay there.

The beautiful poetry of Psalm 91:1 (NKJV) tells us that when we dwell "in the secret place of the Most High" we will "abide under the shadow of the Almighty." In the secret place we'll discover a level of safety and inner stillness that's like nothing we have ever known before. Things may be shaking all around us, but we will have that "peace . . . which surpasses all understanding" (Philippians 4:7 NKJV) because we will be in fellowship with the Lord.

> IN THE SECRET PLACE WE'LL DISCOVER
> A LEVEL OF SAFETY AND INNER STILLNESS
> THAT'S LIKE NOTHING WE HAVE
> EVER KNOWN BEFORE.

In the secret place we'll be at one with him, moving in the Spirit, crucifying the flesh. It's impossible to be nervous or scared in the secret place because we're constantly reminded of how great God is and how much he loves us.

I'm not saying we'll be floating three feet off the ground, totally out of touch with reality. From time to time things will break in that will ruffle the calm, but not for long. No matter what happens, we will know where to go. We will be able to tuck up under God's mighty wing of protection where we can worship him. And as we see him in control, his Spirit will fill us and we will know his perfect peace.

BECOMING OVERCOMERS

The way I see it, there's just no way we can live for long as depressed saints. Look at the disciples and all the things they went through. For instance, Paul was hunted down and thrown into jail, yet he lived a tremendously victorious life in the middle of unbelievable trials. He wasn't afraid of anything that life could throw at him. Jesus was everything to Paul. His relationship with Jesus gave him all he needed to rise above every hard thing he went through in life.

The same thing should be said of us. When Jesus is everything to us, we have all the power we need to rise above whatever trials life sends our way. In the presence of our Lord there is so much joy, so much peace, so much hope, that we can be overcomers in every situation. In fact, Jesus tells us the secret of overcoming trials in John 16:33: "In this world you will have trouble. But take heart! I have overcome the world." We can find tremendous encouragement in the fact that Jesus has already overcome not only our present trials, but our future trials as well. If we'll look to the Lord in every situation, if we'll practice the daily lifestyle of intimate worship, we will find the strength to overcome whatever challenges life brings our way.

An Audience of One

I heard Sheila Walsh say something profound about worship in a concert not long ago. She said that when she sings, no matter how many people are in the audience, she sings before an audience of One. She sings for the Lord. I love that thought!

You know, I believe it's possible to live our whole life like that. To live our life for an audience of One. It's possible to keep Jesus in front of our eyes, in the center of our conscious mind, in the middle of our heart all the time, knowing that he's always with us, knowing that we're always with him.

When we keep the Lord front and center in our mind and our heart, our days will change. Our life will become a life of worship no matter what we're doing. We'll find ourselves blessing the people we live with because we're so aware that Jesus is with us. And when we know he's with us, how can we do anything else but be a blessing to others? We'll find ourselves pulling for the people we work with instead of competing with them. We'll find ourselves free to love in a way that we've never loved before. Loving those who he loves with the love that is his. And the worship that springs forth in us as we live like that will be so natural and beautiful and free that it will truly surprise us!

Is it really possible to become this simple and worshipful and loving no matter what we're doing? It's not only possible; it's nothing short of cooperating with God's perfect purpose for our life. I believe it can happen naturally when we live our everyday life before an audience of One, and that One is the Lord Jesus Christ.

CHAPTER FOUR

WHO BENEFITS FROM WORSHIP?

BENEFITS TO THE LOST

Up to now I've stressed the importance of worship to the worshiper. Obviously those of us who are worshiping will be the ones most affected. But worshipers are not the only ones who benefit from worship. There is also a dying world out there, a world of lost people who benefit from worship happening around them. There are many who don't know the Lord at all and who will only see him in the lives of believers. They will only find him in the faith of those who love him. True worship can be like a lighthouse on a hill to the lost and lonely people of this generation—people who may not even know that they are looking for the Lord.

We can't afford to have a smug, complacent attitude that says, "As long as we are saved and our kids are saved, everything's okay." When we have a heart like the Lord's, we will ache for the lost souls around us. We can't feel

great about being safe when so many are in danger of being lost. And that's

why worship becomes an outreach to souls who need to know our God.

This doesn't even necessarily mean that the worshiping person will

be changing the world with the literal act of worship. But a worshiping

heart will shine through in everything the worshiper does, whether he

> TRUE WORSHIP CAN BE LIKE A LIGHTHOUSE ON
> A HILL TO THE LOST AND LONELY PEOPLE OF
> THIS GENERATION—PEOPLE WHO MAY NOT EVEN
> KNOW THAT THEY ARE LOOKING FOR THE LORD.

or she is worshiping at the time or not. It will show through in his smile,

in the kindness of her words and deeds, in whatever ways the Lord lives

through that person's life. The worshiping heart of a person can touch

the unsaved world in a hundred simple ways every single day by being

Christ to the world.

Benefits to the World

Worshiping is a state of heart that changes the world. It ushers in the kingdom. The person with a worshiping heart goes out into the world and can't help but make a difference everywhere he goes, because he lives not as himself but as Christ living within (see Galatians 2:20). The person with a worshiping heart is tender toward others. She holds a friend accountable to do the right thing when temptation is strong. He steps in and becomes Jesus in every situation. When a person with a worshiping heart comes into the room, the atmosphere seems to change because Jesus is shining through.

Just the other day I went through the drive-through of a restaurant, and when the young man who waited on me recognized who I was, his face just lit up. He started laughing out loud and said, "Praise God! I have been having a really bad day. But I believe the Lord is saying to me right now that everything is going to be okay."

That young guy didn't know me at all, but he knew I was a Christian, so it was like he was getting a kiss from God to see another Christian come into the place where he was working. I laughed out loud, too. Just to see his joy gave me joy and reminded me of who I represent at all times. I pray that he was encouraged to remember that he "can do all things through Christ who strengthens [him]" (Philippians 4:13 NKJV).

When God gives us a worshiping heart, he will lead us into all kinds of opportunities to shine his light on people who we might never see again.

Moving through the world as worshipers, we may make some people a little bit uncomfortable at times. (Jesus made lots of people uncomfortable!) But we will also be able to calm the seas of controversy in others' situations. Our presence will bring healing to broken hearts and broken relationships. When we're willing to have our flesh step aside, when we

> **WHEN GOD GIVES US A WORSHIPING HEART, HE WILL LEAD US INTO ALL KINDS OF OPPORTUNITIES TO SHINE HIS LIGHT ON PEOPLE WHO WE MIGHT NEVER SEE AGAIN.**

invite Jesus to move into the center of our life, exciting things begin to happen! He brings hope to us so that everywhere we go we can bring hope to others. We're like a walking chain reaction when we live as worshipers in an unsaved world.

BENEFITS TO THE LORD

One thing we should remember is that we're really worshiping to benefit and bless the Lord. What a wonder to consider the fact that God blessed us with so many incredible gifts of every kind, and then to top it all off, he blessed us with the gift of worship so that we could turn right around and bless him back by worshiping him!

Worshiping God is what we were created for. And when we worship Him we give him pleasure. The Lord has been dealing with me on that one lately. I want so much for my worship to give him pleasure. I want to live a life that is pleasing to God.

But I have to confess that in my own life I can get busy. It's just unbelievable how a day can slip by me so fast that sometimes I won't even have the thought, *CeCe, did you please your Lord today?* How can that be when he's laid his whole life down for me?

It's so easy for us as human beings to slip into the level of "I, I, I." "What I feel, what I think, what I need." "Self, self, self." No wonder this selfish world is so full of unhappy, dysfunctional people. The Bible tells us that "no flesh should glory in His presence" (1 Corinthians 1:29 NKJV). And if we can't get into his presence, we're never going to find true contentment or happiness. That's why we need to tell our flesh to take a back seat and remember that ultimately, worship is all about the Lord!

CHAPTER FIVE

A WORSHIPING HEART

DEVELOPING HABITS OF THE WORSHIP LIFE

Even though worship feels natural and free, sometimes it's helpful to structure the times and places of our worship so that the busy world doesn't crowd out our time to be with the Lord. We can develop habits of worship just like we develop any other good habits. A great place to start is by using the power of choice that God gives to all of us.

God made us choosers. So begin by choosing to put him first. Choose to surrender your heart. Choose to focus on him. Choose to set aside a certain time in the day for him and him alone.

Never allow yourself to think in terms like "I know I should worship" or "I guess I ought to worship."

Suppose you told your husband, "I know we should get together sometime. I know we ought to spend time together." How do you think that would make him feel? He probably wouldn't get the feeling that you wanted to spend time with him, would he?

Don't let those "should" and "ought" thoughts turn your precious time of worship into a dull obligation. Instead, teach yourself to look forward to every moment you get to spend with the Lord, just as you would look forward to time with your spouse or your best friend. The

> **DON'T LET "SHOULD" AND "OUGHT" THOUGHTS TURN YOUR PRECIOUS TIME OF WORSHIP INTO A DULL OBLIGATION.**

Lord is the very best friend you will ever have. Make the time you spend with him special. And let it delight you just as much as it delights him.

You make dates with your other friends or with your spouse or with your children. Is the God of the universe less worthy of your time? The First Commandment says that the Lord wants to be the most important Person in your life (see Exodus 20:3). Make your very important date with him by setting aside a certain time or times to meet him during the day. Mark those times on your calendar. Then be very intentional about keeping your date with him. You might feel a little shy on your first date. That's the way it is sometimes on first dates, isn't it? But that's okay. It will be exciting and even fun. And soon you'll learn to love meeting him so much you wouldn't miss it for anything. You'll look forward to that special time more than any other time in your day.

AN ALL-DAY-LONG LOVE

Find a time and a place where you can sing to the Lord. Even if the car is the only private place you have, that's okay. Use a CD or tape to sing along with. Or better yet, a melody from your own heart. Yours is the voice he loves.

Find a time during the day to read part of the Word and think about it. Meditate on it. Let it soak into your spirit. And you might ask the Lord in your heart, *Lord, now what did you mean by that?* Listen to him. He'll answer you. And soon you'll find that you know his voice so well. And you'll find you've got these little conversations going on between the two of you all day long. Just like any other two people in love. And oh how you'll love the all-day-long love he has for you!

You know, I wouldn't want my husband to speak to me just once during the day. I wouldn't want him to have the kind of attitude that would say to me, "Well, CeCe, I said 'Good morning' at breakfast. Isn't that enough?" But some of us treat God like that. We act like if we prayed in the morning, that ought to satisfy God for the whole day.

But what God wants is a deep, intimate love relationship. And once we taste that kind of relationship with him, we won't be satisfied with anything less. Once we come close and taste his goodness, once we have a daily diet of his mercy, once we get used to the little ways he wants to delight us with his love, we'll never want to move outside the circle of his presence.

Put the Lord at the Center

It's true that the world will try to distract us. It always does. So when I see myself getting sidetracked by the world or getting wrapped up in myself, I've just got to say, "Stop!" I've got to sit down and rethink my whole life and my whole schedule.

I start by putting the Lord at the very center of my schedule. Then I do away with everything except what is truly necessary, and I try to fit those truly necessary things around him. I make sure that I have time for his Word and prayer and worshiping him first, and then I fit the

> ONCE WE COME CLOSE AND TASTE GOD'S GOODNESS, ONCE WE HAVE A DAILY DIET OF HIS MERCY, WE'LL NEVER WANT TO MOVE OUTSIDE THE CIRCLE OF HIS PRESENCE.

other things in. He's the one true, indispensable thing in my life. And I know that without him I can't make it. Without him nothing else is right. Nothing satisfies like the love of the Lord.

The reason that's true is that he is what I was made for. I was made to love him and worship him and lift him up and build his kingdom and enjoy being in his presence and give him pleasure forever. If I miss out on that, I miss out on the very purpose of my life. So I'd better get it right. And if I get that part right, he'll help me get all the other things taken care of. If I take care of his business, he'll help me take care of my business.

WRITE IT ALL DOWN

Write out your choice to put Jesus first. You may want to buy a notebook or a journal to write your decision in, or write it on your word processor or Palm Pilot so you can see it in black and white. Make Jesus first in your life with worship and the Word. Then fit other essentials like family, church commitments, and work around the Lord.

We are very literal people. Seeing things written down helps us get them in perspective. Don't let a busy, noisy world steal you away from the One who knows you best and loves you most.

PLAN TO PLEASE HIM

God is a God of order. When our world is full of chaos, it's hard to give him our best. When our world is orderly, God blesses it. So don't give the Lord your scraps of time and attention. Look at your day and create a special window of time and an orderly space where you can meet the Lord you love. Give him your best. He will honor that.

The way you come before God is very important. Your life may be filled with so much clutter that your mind and heart may be reflecting that clutter when you approach your Father in worship. It may be time to clear out and put your whole house in order so that you can bring to your God a heart that will please Him. Pleasing the Lord must come first. But often in order to please him, you must plan to please him. Make a plan in your life and in your day so that you will have the time and space and order that you need to reflect the love in your heart.

No Third Party

I visited with a dear friend, Mother Stacks, not long ago. She told me that the Lord had been dealing with her on the issue of "no third party." What did she mean by "no third party"? God was simply saying to her that he wanted to be first in her life.

He knew she had good Christian friends and he knew she enjoyed corporate worship and he knew she relied on her pastor's wisdom. But in spite of the fact that those were all good relationships, he didn't want anything to take the place of her one-on-one relationship with him. She knew that's what God meant when he whispered "no third party" in her spirit. You see, our God really is a jealous God and he wants to be the one who is closest and most important to his children.

Sometimes we get very attached to a certain prayer partner, or we begin to rely on a certain small group. Our Christian brothers and sisters are gifts to us from the Lord, but we should never lose sight of the fact that the Lord always wants to be first in our life. He wants us to run to him first with our prayers and our news and our needs and our worship and everything in our heart. He wants us to lean on him totally. He's waiting for that kind of love from each one of us. He longs for it.

In the outer courts we are with our friends, our loved ones, our colaborers. They are the ones we pray with and confess our faults to and lift up in prayer. But the closer we get to the holy of holies—the closer we get to the Throne Room—the less we are aware of others and the more we are focused on the Lord. Our eyes are on him alone. Our heart is centered on him. Our songs are lifted to him.

The more focused we become on the Lord, the more he is able to do the things that only he can do. True worship creates an atmosphere where healing takes place, where deliverance takes place, and where the words of Scripture take on a deeper meaning. In the inner court, for instance, we become more able to "not worry about tomorrow" (Matthew 6:34), for there it suddenly seems possible to dwell in the moment. In the inner court we find ourselves more able to "set [our] mind on things above," and not on things below (Colossians 3:2 NKJV). The closer we move to the Lord in the Throne Room, the more his truth becomes our reality.

> **TRUE WORSHIP CREATES AN ATMOSPHERE WHERE HEALING TAKES PLACE, WHERE DELIVERANCE TAKES PLACE, AND WHERE THE WORDS OF SCRIPTURE TAKE ON A DEEPER MEANING.**

REHEARSING FOR ETERNITY

As we come closer to the Lord in worship, our heart is really rehearsing for that higher place where we'll someday see him face to face. But the truth is that all of life to one who loves the Lord should be a rehearsal for eternity. We should be living what I call the "worship lifestyle" every day.

The worship lifestyle puts into practice the habits and attitudes and actions we won't be ashamed of when we stand before the Lord. Attitudes like gratitude and joy, inner peace, patience, faithfulness, self-control, denying ourselves, and carrying each other's burdens. Now is the time to be building ourselves up in the spirit man. Now is the time to be preparing our spirit man for the kind of life we'll carry with us throughout eternity. The more we exercise the spirit man, the stronger he will become. The more we ignore and deny the flesh, the less power it will have to control us. This is living the worship lifestyle.

CHAPTER SIX

MOVING INTO THE LORD'S PRESENCE

Sometimes someone will ask me whether there is any special order to the things I say or sing when I worship in the Throne Room. Every time I go to the Lord I listen to him and let him lead me. Every time is different. Here are some things the Lord will sometimes have me do.

CONFESSING

It's wonderful to know that our God knows us inside out, and he loves us without holding anything back. So if any sin is coming between God and me, usually the first thing he will do is show me that sin and give me a chance to confess it so he can clean up my heart. What a blessing to stand before him white as snow!

First John 1:9 says, "If we confess our sins, he is faithful and just and will forgive us our sins and purify us from all unrighteousness." Nothing shocks God. He's seen it all. And he's ready to forgive us the minute we're ready to confess. Our part is the little part (confessing). His part is the big part (forgiving and cleaning us up). So the sooner we get it over with, the sooner we can get on with worshiping him.

Surrendering

Surrendering can be defined as the spirit of humility. It is being willing to open our hands and let go of every distracting thing that is keeping us from focusing totally on the Lord. We quiet our spirit. We center our mind. We turn our heart to him. We don't rush into his presence with a million thoughts and ideas and conflicting feelings whirling around in our head. We release everything that is fighting against the fact that we are his. We turn the eyes of our heart toward the reality of his lordship and come face to face with the fact that we are nothing apart from him.

Sometimes surrendering involves simply waiting on the Lord. I remember once hearing Andraé Crouch talk about "waiting on the Lord." He said he had a life-changing revelation when he realized that to wait on the Lord is not always done in terms of time. Many times when we wait on the Lord, we are more like a waitress or a waiter. It involves serving him. This is where the term *servanthood* comes in.

When we wait on the Lord as his servants, we acknowledge him as Lord over everything. We come to him saying, "Lord, how can I serve you today?"

> **THE QUESTION WE SHOULD BE BRINGING TO GOD IN WORSHIP IS, "FATHER, HOW CAN I BRING YOU GLORY?" THIS IS THE POSTURE OF SURRENDER.**

But isn't it amazing how easy it is to go to church and leave, never once having had that thought? We can sit through the whole service, and the only waiting we do is waiting for some encouraging word for ourselves. We're thinking about how the Lord can serve us instead of how we can serve him.

The question we should be bringing to him in worship is, "Father, how can I bring you glory?" This is the posture of surrender. The Lord wants to shine through everything we do. What we discover when we become worshipers is that everything we do should reflect his love and his life. Whatever we do for him will bring him glory when we offer him a surrendered heart—a heart that waits to serve him.

LOVING THE LORD

Once you are surrendered, you can rest in God's presence. The reality of his nearness becomes very real as you still your heart before him. Just begin to worship him with your own words or find a passage in the Bible, maybe one of the psalms that you love, and use it as a love song to the Lord.

Or you might want to worship him by lifting up one of his many names. A few of those names that are found in the Bible are listed below:

Our Redeemer *(Isaiah 47:4)*

Our Mighty One *(Isaiah 33:21)*

Our Refuge and Strength *(Psalm 46:1)*

Rock of Our Salvation *(Psalm 95:1)*

My Shepherd *(Psalm 23:1)*

Eternal God *(Genesis 21:33)*

The Consuming Fire *(Isaiah 33:14)*

Alpha and Omega *(Revelation 1:8)*

Bread of Life *(John 6:48)*

The Resurrection and the Life *(John 11:25)*

Bright Morning Star *(Revelation 22:16)*

The Gate *(John 10:7, 9)*

The One and Only *(John 1:14, 18)*

The Radiance of God's Glory *(Hebrews 1:3)*

The Way *(John 14:6)*

Prince of Peace *(Isaiah 9:6)*

My Friend *(Jeremiah 3:4)*

Immanuel, God with us *(Matthew 1:23)*

Wonderful Counselor *(Isaiah 9:6)*

Or choose other words that mean the most to you and begin saying those words softly or singing them. Here are some words that I love to sing to the Lord: holy, lovely, worthy, Savior, righteous, beautiful, faithful, wonderful, powerful, friend. Lift your words up as an offering. Realize that the One to whom you are singing loves you totally. He has invited you here. Be at peace. Rest in him. Relax in his presence. No one is grading you or expecting you to get it "right."

U S I N G   M U S I C

You might want to sing the simplest song you can think of, like "Jesus Loves Me," with your open hands on your lap. See Jesus there with you. Lift your face to him and feel the warmth of his smile.

You might want to play a worship tape or CD and sing along. Keep a collection of your favorite worship CDs near your CD player so that you can reach for the one God puts on your heart each day. You may find yourself creating your own harmony or words when you sing along. Or if you are alone, you might want to dance. Give your voice and your movements to the Lord. He loves you. He sees you as beautiful. Offer your worship to him.

Music is not worship itself, but music is a means of carrying our worship. Lifting our hands is another way our worship is carried up to the Lord (see 1 Timothy 2:8).

Music can do work in the spiritual realm. Think of when Saul called David, the shepherd boy, to come and play his harp. When David would play, the evil spirit would leave Saul alone (see 1 Samuel 16:14–23). Music, in the hands of God's servant, waged warfare against the spirit that was tormenting the king.

> ## MUSIC IS NOT WORSHIP ITSELF,
> ## BUT MUSIC IS A MEANS OF
> ## CARRYING OUR WORSHIP.

God seems to have spread the love of music throughout the hearts of all people. When I travel abroad, I am amazed to see the power of music in all the different countries, in all the different languages, and in all the different cultures. I believe that's because God has given music a universal power to touch the human heart.

CHAPTER SEVEN

WORSHIP AND
SPIRITUAL WARFARE

A DESPERATE NEED FOR WORSHIP

I realize that some churches don't teach their members how to worship, how to cry out, how to lift their hands. If your church isn't a church that teaches these things, it's my prayer that you will at least find a worshiping prayer group or Bible study group where you will be encouraged in the ways of worship. All of us have a desperate need to worship. Not just so we can get a warm, "glowy" feeling inside. It's so much more important than that. In a world like the one we live in, the ways of worship are the weapons of our warfare.

No matter what situation we're in, when we praise the Lord, we bring amazing spiritual power into that situation. The Bible tells us that "the garment of praise" will lift "the spirit of heaviness" (Isaiah 61:3 KJV). It tells us that the "weapons of our warfare are not carnal, but mighty through God to the pulling down of strong holds" (2 Corinthians 10:4 KJV).

True worship is the lifestyle of loving the Lord, of setting our heart on him and putting him first. As we love him and surrender to him daily in worship, we'll see the battles he can win on our behalf.

DEEP THINGS OF THE SPIRIT

Today more than ever, we need to be aware of the deep things of the Spirit. Now more than ever, we need to worship the Lord in the secret place. Years ago maybe we could get away with paddling around in shallow spiritual water. But that won't make it now. When I listen to the news and see what's going on in the world, I realize how much we need God's protection against the evil that has been so freely set loose in this dark age. Without worship we are defenseless and uncovered in the spirit realm. Just going to church is not enough. We need the power of intimate worship and an intimate relationship with the Lord.

WHAT OUR CHILDREN FACE

Our children are the ones I feel for most strongly. They are facing worse things than we ever dreamed of at their ages. That's why we've got to help them get ready for what's coming. They've got to press into God now.

I told my eighteen-year-old son, Alvin, just the other day, "Alvin, what took me thirty-eight years to get, you've got to get now. You won't make it if you don't. You don't have any choice."

I said, "The Lord is more than able to do it. I'm not saying this to make you afraid, but this is to let you know that you have to take hold now. Because you guys are facing things we didn't have to face. What's on television, what's the norm now—those things weren't even tolerated when we were kids. Everything's coming at you guys now. They're saying you can't pray. They're taking spiritual things away from you. You've got to have it on the inside, Alvin. You've got to get connected."

I told him, "You can't ride on what I do. It's got to be your own faith, your own relationship with God. You don't have the luxury of playing games. Alvin, you have to be on fire for the Lord. Lukewarm isn't going to get it."

A Song with Attitude!

The devil's work has always been "to steal and kill and destroy" (John 10:10), but it just seems to me that he's been putting in a lot of overtime these days. It seems like he's been working harder at being evil and stealing the good than I can ever remember in the past. The enemy realizes that this age is almost over, so he's making every minute count for evil. He's not taking a break; he's not relaxing. He's pulling out every trick in the book. The level of sin that I'm seeing around me in the world is so much more obvious and deliberate than at any other time since I've been alive. I'm seeing a level of unashamed evil in people that I can hardly believe.

I wrote a song for an earlier CD called "Devil, Get Out of My House!" And I wrote it with an attitude. I remember getting angry when I was writing that song. Because I think a lot of us put up with more than we have to. We need to get mad. It's time to stop tolerating so much.

If we're not submerged in the Holy Spirit, how in the world do we expect to have the power we need to stand up against everything that's coming against us? If we're not spending time in the Lord's presence, it's easy to forget who we are and what our rights are. We need to remind ourselves who we are in him. As Christians, we have all authority in Jesus Christ over ourselves and our marriages and our children. We are the heirs of a powerful King. And we don't have to put up with the evil and the lies that the enemy's been throwing around at us and at our families.

We don't have to be shaking and quaking in our boots. Satan is not the one in power. In the name of Jesus and by the power of his blood,

> **IF YOU'VE LOST SIGHT OF WHO YOU ARE IN CHRIST, YOU MAY NEED TO WORSHIP YOUR WAY BACK INTO CLARITY.**

we can tell the enemy to take his lies and get out of our house, and take his hands off of our children and our marriage and get lost! It's time to take back any ground that he's gained. And it's time to reclaim everything that is ours in the name of the Lord Jesus Christ and by the blood of the Lamb.

So if you've lost sight of who you are in Christ, you may need to worship your way back into clarity. And as you worship the Lord, let him show you with perfect 20/20 Spirit vision who he is and who you are in him.

THE POWER OF THE LORD'S HOLINESS

However evil the evil may be, however dark the darkness may get, keep this in mind: It can never compete with the level and the power of the Lord's holiness! There is no match. No competition. The Lord's amazing brilliance and power and purity are so blindingly beautiful that they can outshine anything that the world tries to hold up in the face of them. Demons tremble at the sound of his name. Just say "Jesus," and the realm of the enemy is put to flight. The sound of that name melts the force of evil. Isn't that amazing?

You may be wondering what I wonder at times. If demons tremble at his name, then why don't we walk in victory all the time? What happens to us that holds us back? What's the problem? The problem is this: We move in and out of a lukewarm faith. We don't stay 100 percent sold out for Jesus the way we should.

In fact, it sometimes seems to me that there are a whole lot more people who are 100 percent sold out to the devil than there are people who are 100 percent sold out to God. I look at some people I know in the entertainment field and I get the sense that they are totally sold out to the darkness. They are bold. They'll say anything. They'll do anything. They have no shame whatsoever. The enemy has won these people over 100 percent. They are gung-ho for the enemy!

TIME TO BE SOLD OUT FOR THE LORD

Isn't it time for every one of us who wears the name "Christian" to be totally sold out for the Lord? We can't afford to be shy about our faith. We can't stand back in the shadows not wanting to offend anybody with our beliefs when there is so much blatant evil slapping us in the face everywhere we go. It's time to stand up and boldly be counted as Christians.

I'm not saying we have to wear a billboard that says, "Repent, brothers!" I'm just saying that we need to be willing to speak Christ's name when it's time to speak his name. Because if we belong to Jesus, it's not about us. It's about him. It's about making a difference for his kingdom before he returns. We will never know whose life will be changed for eternity by that one thing we're willing to open our mouth and say.

Lately I have had more boldness than I've ever had before. I just know that every time I speak out for Jesus in the Spirit I'm actually tearing down some corner of Satan's kingdom. That's why I'm not willing to be a polite, wallflower Christian anymore. It's too late for that. If we're going to stand in this evil world, we're going to have to be totally committed, over-the-edge, on-fire worshipers who are constantly in communication with the Lord—morning, noon, and night. The kind of worshipers who know that he's our Song and he's our Rock and he's our Reason for everything. He's the River flowing nonstop through our heart.

We need to be the kind of worshipers who know that we can get everything we need in worship. We get healed in worship, we get fed in worship, and we get cleansed in worship, because when we are worshiping we are plugged into the power source. We're plugged into the God who knows exactly what we need.

FANS FOR JESUS

I remember a time in this country when talking about the Lord like this would make some people laugh behind your back, or tease you and call you a "Jesus freak" or a "holy roller" or a fanatic.

The word *fanatic* comes from the same word as the word *fan*. You can't live in this sports-crazy country and not know what a fan is. Every weekend in the fall there are stadiums all over the country full of people who howl and yell and scream and pay good money to watch two

> **WE WILL NEVER KNOW WHOSE LIFE WILL BE CHANGED FOR ETERNITY BY THAT ONE THING WE'RE WILLING TO OPEN OUR MOUTH AND SAY.**

teams of men in uniforms kick and throw a pigskin around a field. They don't mind being fanatics for football. But some of those same people would be embarrassed to death to worship the Lord, to lift their hands, to speak the name of Jesus in a public place. They would consider that just too fanatical.

Isn't it about time that we became "fans" for Jesus Christ? Isn't it about time that we stepped over the line and let the world know in no uncertain terms whose side we are on? We need to order our life in such a way that we start pushing back the tide of the evil day with the strength of our faith and the power of our worship no matter what name somebody decides to give us. Let's be a little bit fanatical for the Lord!

WORSHIP AS WARFARE

We'll never be a real threat to the enemy until we understand that our job as worshipers is to lift up our Lord so that he can draw all men to himself. That's how we set ourselves in opposition to evil.

> WE'LL NEVER BE A REAL THREAT TO THE ENEMY UNTIL WE UNDERSTAND THAT OUR JOB AS WORSHIPERS IS TO LIFT UP OUR LORD SO THAT HE CAN DRAW ALL MEN TO HIMSELF.

I'm not afraid of the enemy. I'm tired of him. I hate him. I know that he has already been defeated on Calvary. But I want to do everything in my power every day that I'm alive to make things rough for him on Planet Earth. And I know that as a true worshiper, I'm a true weapon. Whenever I'm in the act of worshiping, I can go in and snatch everything the enemy has stolen. I can do that in the powerful name of the Lord Jesus Christ and by his authority. So I have made up my mind that I'm not going to let Satan gain another inch of territory while I'm on my watch.

WAYS OF WARFARE

Here are some of the ways that I operate as a warrior and a worshiper in the army of the Lord.

(1) I Worship Immediately

To begin with, when things come up, even if they seem to be bad or negative, I begin immediately to praise the Lord. Even if I have no idea how they are going to work out, even if I'm hurting, I start to focus in on him and I begin to worship him. I have no doubt that he is a good God, so I choose not to look at the circumstances but to look at his faithfulness and his mercy. In his Word he has told me to "always [give] thanks to God the Father for everything, in the name of our Lord Jesus Christ" (Ephesians 5:20). And so I begin doing just that. Not focusing on the problem, but focusing on the solution. Because I know that he is the solution, regardless of what the problem is.

I begin to turn my heart toward him, giving him praise and honor and glory and worship. With my lips and my heart I tell him how great and good and glorious he is. And I say, "Father, you know what's happening and you know the solution because you're the God of everything, and you are the solution. I trust you with this situation, just as I trust you with everything else in this life." And as I tell him these things, strength begins to flow into me. Because he is strength. There is no weakness in him. Then I begin to feel steady and calm and filled with trust because I know that he is in control. Whether it's an illness in my family or two planes flying into the Twin Towers in New York City. Whatever the scope of the problem, I know he's greater than any negative thing that's going on. I can trust him with my life and my world.

As a matter of fact, the 9-11 tragedy in New York City is a very real example of a specific time when I worshiped instead of panicking. My flight had just landed in Chicago, and the pilot announced over the intercom that one of the Twin Towers in New York City had been hit by a plane and that terrorist activity was suspected.

My first thought was, Jesus is coming back soon. It was so funny how I was immediately in touch with the eternal part of who I am. Suddenly nothing in the earthly realm seemed to matter. (The diet I had been on, for instance. Forget it! Give me the biggest cheeseburger you have! I might be taken out of here any minute!)

But another thing that was so interesting about it all was that I was very concerned about what was going on in New York and I was praying for the people there, but at the same time I had a tremendous peace because I knew God was in control. I remember later that day a television announcer said that one of the next targets of the terrorists might be the Sears Tower in Chicago, where I was. And a little prayer flickered across my heart. *Lord,* I prayed, *I don't have any idea what's going to happen next, but I know this one thing: If I get taken out, I'm going home to be with you. And I worship you as the Lord who is in control of all things.*

What a blessed assurance we have when we know the Lord! The enemy cannot shake our peace. We can worship our way right out of almost any panic situation. The peace comes not in knowing all the answers to what will happen. The peace comes in knowing the Lord. When you know him, you already know that the result is victory. As the Bible says, "If God is for us, who can be against us?" (Romans 8:31).

(2) I Worship When I Feel Wronged

Even in situations when I feel that someone has done something against me, instead of wasting time feeling hurt or betrayed, I immediately begin to worship. When I worship the Lord in this situation, it never fails. I begin to remember what he went through for me. I remember how he died for me when I had betrayed him. And as I focus on his sacrifice, I am suddenly overwhelmed with love for him. That is when I find that he gives me compassion for the person or persons who have hurt me. And my whole attitude changes from "me, me, me" to "Oh God, how good you are! After all you've done for me that I didn't deserve, please Lord, give me your heart so I can make it through these hurt feelings. And Lord, help me to forgive this person. Help me to love as you love."

(3) I Worship When I Need to Be Steady and Strong

No matter what kind of spiritual battle I find myself in, I have come to see that worship is strength to the worshiper and frustration to the enemy. Worship is also my greatest weapon against fear and my greatest ally against the unknown. Again and again I have found it to be a source of power against all of the enemy's wiles. Why? Simply because when I worship, I automatically go into the secret place, the place that all hell cannot shake. Worship releases power into every situation, because when I worship I am focusing on nothing but light—no darkness, no weakness, and no fear.

> **WORSHIP IS STRENGTH**
>
> **TO THE WORSHIPER AND**
>
> **FRUSTRATION TO THE ENEMY.**

We are living in such volatile times. Things change around us so fast that our greatest help and healing comes to us when we focus our heart on the God who is unchanging, the God who is "the same yesterday and today and forever" (Hebrews 13:8). As we worship him, we are able to face an unsteady age with a heart that is steady and secure, "rooted and established" in his all-powerful love (Ephesians 3:17).

(4) I Worship on the Front Lines As a Priest and a Warrior

I think there was a time when many church members subconsciously saw their role in the body of Christ as benchwarmers. They went to the church house to sit on the pew and hear what the man of God would say that week. But we can't afford to think that way anymore. This is a totally different season.

I am excited to be alive right now. I'm excited about this time in the world when I realize that the Lord has called every one of us into "active duty." We are called to take our place on the front lines in this war with the enemy. Every one of us needs to recognize the active role we've got to play in the Lord's kingdom.

> EVERY MEMBER OF THE BODY OF CHRIST MUST
> SEE HIMSELF OR HERSELF AS A MINISTER,
> A WORSHIPER, A PRIEST, AND A WARRIOR IN THE
> SPIRITUAL WARFARE OF THIS AGE.

We can't designate a few paid musicians to be our professional worshipers. We're all worshipers before our God. We can't designate our pastor to pray for us. We're all prayer warriors. Every member of the body of

Christ must see himself or herself as a minister, a worshiper, a priest, and a warrior in the spiritual warfare of this age. No one can live without a one-on-one relationship with the Lord. Every one of us has to be empowered to go out and win this dying world for our Lord's eternal kingdom before he comes again. This is a high calling and an exciting place to stand! Equip us, Lord, as your church!

CHAPTER EIGHT

HOW WORSHIP CHANGES THINGS

WORSHIP CHANGES THE HEART ATTITUDE

One thing that encourages me to worship is to see the ways that worship is changing me and others around me. The most exciting thing that has begun to happen in my life as a worshiper is that I am finding myself able to maintain a worshipful heart attitude for longer and longer periods of time. For instance, sometimes when I'm alone doing the laundry I'll find myself using the quiet time to be with the Lord and worship him. I've learned that I don't have to "pop" in and out of the Spirit all day long. I can stay in a grateful spirit of worship during more and more of the day if I keep my heart focused on the Lord.

WORSHIP COMES FORTH IN
GOOD AND BAD TIMES

Lately I find that my spirit moves quickly to worship even when unpleasant or bad things are happening. And I pray that eventually no matter how hard life is pressing me, nothing will come out of my heart but worship. And nothing will come out of my mouth but, "Lord, I trust you. You're wonderful. I worship you."

That should be the goal of every true worshiper. We should look at every day as a challenge, praying, "Lord, this day I choose to stay before you in a worshipful heart attitude all day long. Thank you for being in control."

I believe that as we grow in the worship life, this heart attitude will begin to be in us more and more. It will be who we are. It will be our true self coming forth in every situation, good or bad, because it's been cultivated day by day as we've worshiped our Savior in all kinds of situations. It will have shaped us as his people. We won't constantly be asking him for this and that. We'll just be living out our life before him quietly and joyfully, aware of his presence and surrendered to his Spirit.

Worship Leads Us to God's Perfect Purposes for Our Life

The only way we can really learn about ourselves and be all we were created to be is by getting to know the One who created us. God knows us better than we know ourselves, and he loves us more than anyone else. If we could only get a God's-eye glimpse of ourselves, we would be totally healed and set right within, because God sees us perfectly. He sees us as were designed to be, walking in the purposes he made us for.

> **The only way we can really learn about ourselves and be all we were created to be is by getting to know the One who created us.**

When we truly love the Lord, our deepest longing is to find and to follow his perfect will for our life because we know that nothing else will fulfill us.

When you look at the people in the world who are living apart from God, it's easy to see that we human beings don't know the first thing about what will make us happy, or else we wouldn't be so sad. We don't know who we are, or else we wouldn't be so confused. Men trying to be women. Women trying to be men. Adults trying to be children. Children trying to be adults. Everybody trying to be something they're not.

Only in God do we find the true purpose that will bring inner joy. When we are moving in God's purposes, he gets the glory, others get blessed, and we find our heart's fulfillment. There is such an urgency in this age for the members of the body of Christ to be working in their purposes, accomplishing the things that we were created to do for the kingdom before the Lord returns. Worship is a means for uniting us as God's family and leading us to the things he has set out for us to do corporately and individually. As we stand before him surrendered, he can speak to the hearts of his children.

WORSHIP LIFTS JESUS UP

It's an exciting thing to belong to a worshiping church because we can look around and can see a whole body of believers doing what they were created to do. The first and most obvious thing we were created to do is to worship. When we're worshiping God, we're lifting him up. Jesus said in the Bible that when he is lifted up, he will draw all men to himself (see John 12:32). The Lord is still in the business of drawing people to himself.

You know, we get so busy trying to draw people to him ourselves that we forget that's not our job. That's his job. Our job is just to lift him up, which is exactly what we do in worship. If we'll just lift him up in worship, he'll draw people to himself.

Sometimes in our churches we'd rather create another committee or another program that glorifies our hard work rather than glorifying the Lord. I believe that Jesus would like to see us get back to doing it his

---

**SOMETIMES IN OUR CHURCHES
WE'D RATHER CREATE ANOTHER COMMITTEE
OR ANOTHER PROGRAM THAT
GLORIFIES OUR HARD WORK
RATHER THAN GLORIFYING THE LORD.**

---

way. He'd like to see us spend less time emphasizing our "works" and more time lifting him up in worship. Because when we're lifting him up, that's when he can draw people to himself.

Worship Allows the Lord to Show Us the Truth about Ourselves

The closer we get to the Lord when we're worshiping, the closer we get to his light. "In him there is no darkness at all" (1 John 1:5). There is only light. And in that light everything about us is exposed. Because of our surrender to his love, the Lord is able to show us things in ourselves that please him as well as things that need changing. All of them are revealed in the light of his perfection. And when we draw near to him, our aim is always to please him. Because of his great love for us, what he shows us isn't painful. We can take it. And nothing else matters to us but becoming the person that he wants us to become.

CHAPTER NINE

WORSHIP AS A HERITAGE

A DESTINY FOR GOD'S CHILDREN

Whether we realize it or not, all of us as God's children have inherited a need to worship God. It is our destiny. It may be buried deep down inside where we can't see it or feel it, but it's there. It's the purpose of every person. Each of us is set down in a certain place in this world, and God is even now using that place, wherever it is, to develop each of us into a worshiper.

Even if you see your background as a negative one, I strongly believe that the Lord can and will use you as a worshiper, if you'll let him, to break those negative strongholds over your family. He will use you as a worshiper to draw his power into your family so that he can heal whatever has been wounded or broken.

> EACH OF US IS SET DOWN IN A CERTAIN PLACE IN
>
> THIS WORLD, AND GOD IS EVEN NOW USING
>
> THAT PLACE, WHEREVER IT IS,
>
> TO DEVELOP EACH OF US INTO A WORSHIPER.

If you come from a positive place of wholeness and faith, he'll use you as a worshiper to multiply that faith and spread it to the next generation. The very fact that you are reading this book lets me know that he is already planting a seed for good in your life and in the lives of your family members. He is stirring up in you an excitement about worship and what it can mean to you and your family.

EXAMPLES IN MY FAMILY

It's easy for me to see how I have been affected by the family I was born into. Last year my parents celebrated their fiftieth wedding anniversary! That's quite a milestone. I have to say that my parents taught us by living their faith in front of us. They were great examples of what it is to be

Christians. They weren't perfect, but they were great at asking our forgiveness when they made mistakes. They taught us how to pray together, how to be forgiving, and how to apply God's Word to the problems in our lives. I know now how important it was for me to have two parents who loved the Lord, who loved each other, who loved me, who stayed together, and who prayed over us.

I'm also thankful to the Lord that I have two parents who loved music the way they did. Music was one ingredient in my childhood that shaped me and brought me into my life's purpose. All ten of us children loved to sing, and we sang constantly. I think we would have gotten into a lot more fights than we did if we had not been a musical family. We couldn't fight when we were singing, and we were singing all the time!

My parents didn't have a lot of material things when they started out fifty years ago, but they had each other. The Lord was their Rock, and they made a good home for us.

We always went to church as a family. In the beginning it was because our parents made us do it. But little by little we came to love the church ourselves. And there came a time when each of us had to develop a personal relationship with the Lord in our own heart. That's something no parent can spoon-feed a child. Each person has to own it for himself or herself.

SPIRITUAL BLESSINGS

Now as Alvin and I raise our wonderful son, Alvin III (eighteen), and our precious daughter, Ashley (sixteen), I know that I'm building on the bedrock of parenting that I had as a child. There's not a day that I don't thank the Lord for the family I had growing up.

When I look at where my father and my mother came from in the world and how the Lord saved them, when I think about their background and what the Lord brought them through, I just have to be a little

> **WORSHIPING THE LORD HAS THE POWER TO BREAK THE CURSE OF WHAT HAS GONE BEFORE IN A FAMILY.**

bit in awe. It's a powerful example to me of how worshiping the Lord has the power to break the curse of what has gone before in a family.

My parents decided to marry even though they were both from broken homes. They decided that they were going to live holy lives and raise their kids in holiness. I can clearly see the blessings that have come to my brothers and sisters and me because of that decision. I believe that their choice to be a sold-out, worshiping family has reaped spiritual blessings for me and my siblings, as well as for my children. And there are blessings in store for my children's children.

I couldn't be more positive that introducing Jesus into the home I grew up in, and worshiping him and putting him first, gave my parents the authority they needed to break the curses of the enemy over our family. It's like they drew a line with the blood of Christ and said, "In the name of Jesus, the curse stops here, Satan! No more!"

I don't think there is anything on this earth any more important than a God-centered family. By "God-centered," I mean a family in which the parents have made a commitment to the Lord and to each other. It's true that Christian families go through hard times just like every other family. But there is one fundamental difference. The Lord promises that he will "never leave you nor forsake you" (Deuteronomy 31:6). And that is a promise that he keeps.

> I DON'T THINK THERE IS ANYTHING ON THIS
> EARTH ANY MORE IMPORTANT THAN A
> GOD-CENTERED FAMILY, A FAMILY IN WHICH
> THE PARENTS HAVE MADE A COMMITMENT
> TO THE LORD AND TO EACH OTHER.

I just can't imagine living without God in my life. I can't imagine taking on the responsibilities of a family without having the Lord at the center of it all. I know people do it, but I sometimes wonder how they make it through.

WORSHIPING INFLUENCES

My mother, Delores Winans, is a beautiful lady. She's a wonderful example to me in so many ways, and she truly loves the Lord.

But I'd have to say that the person who has influenced me as a worshiper more than any other is my father, David Winans. Even though Dad and I have very different styles of worship, we both have "worshiping hearts."

I have my quiet, focused moments. But not Dad. No way! He's mostly pretty loud and really funny. But the truth is, all you ever hear come out of his mouth is some kind of praise phrase on how crazy he is about the Lord. He just can't stop praising his Savior!

He'll say things like, "Oh, he's wonderful" or, "Oh, I really love him." And, "Isn't that just like my Jesus!" He's an exalter. He exalts God and he trusts God. He's a fireball of a worshiper! I watched that as a kid and it made a big impression on me.

Actually, when I was little, I thought he was probably crazy because I'd wake up in the middle of the night and I could hear him praising God. His praise is pretty noisy. He claps his hands and shouts things like, "Oh, glory to God! Hallelujah!" It could scare a little kid to death! But I got used to it pretty quick. And I realized that that's just the way he expressed himself. He always had praise on his lips. He does to this day. He's just totally in love with the Lord.

I remember during my concerts, I could always hear him shouting out in the crowd and I'd know exactly where he was sitting in the audience. And I'd kind of laugh to myself. But I thank God for it now, because my father has taught me so much about praise and worship. He always said that God inhabits the praises of his people (see Psalm 22:3). So I always knew that God wasn't very far away from my dad!

He always said to me, "CeCe, God loves to be praised! He loves to be worshiped! He loves to be talked about! He loves to be loved! He loves to be boasted on!" So that's what my dad does. That's his life's work. In fact, that's his life!

As I look at him now, I realize that my dad is a total original. (Well, I realize that each one of us is an original, but some of us just seem more original than others!) And I realize that, more than anybody else, he has been my example.

THE FAITH WE LEARNED

Several years ago, my brother Ronald's heart ruptured on the operating table, and God literally brought him back from the dead. Something I've come to realize is that if God had decided to take Ronald in that operating room instead of miraculously healing him the way he did, the Winans family was going to praise him anyway. Because we knew God was worthy to be praised no matter what happened. That was the way our parents had lived their lives in front of us, and that was the faith we had learned from them.

But they also taught us not to give up and to keep praying until God made the final decision. So that was what we did that day in the hospital—that wonderful day that my brother was raised from the dead!

The faith that we learned from my parents taught me something else that means everything to me. It taught me what a marriage looks like. How a husband and a wife stay together. And take their children to church whether those children want to go or not. And how they tell their children, "As for me and my household, we will serve the LORD" (Joshua 24:15). I am so grateful for the faith I learned from my parents.

SECTION
TWO

SONGS ON
THE *THRONE ROOM* CD

A ROMANTIC RECORD

I have to say, before I even talk about any single song on the *Throne Room* project, that this is a romantic CD. The term *romantic* may surprise you. If it does, it's because we've allowed the world to take the words *love* and *romance* and give a worldly definition to them.

Well, I'm taking those words back. I'm repossessing them, because this record is like a love letter to the Lord I love. The concepts of "love" and "romance" originated with the Father. They were his ideas in the first place. His yearning for an intimate relationship with each of us is his yearning for pure romance in which our worship is more captivating and exciting than most of us have ever allowed it to be. I pray that as you

listen to these songs you will allow yourself to come to the Lord with a

pure and romantic heart of love toward him.

PART ONE:
SONGS OF WORSHIP AND REFLECTION

The first part of the CD, the first eight songs, are songs that I believe could be sung in the very Throne Room of the Father himself, because they're not about me or you. They're not about what we're going through. They're not even about what God does for us, his children. They're just about who he is and what he is. And there is tremendous power and strength in singing about that.

I've recorded lots of different kinds of songs in my singing career. And I have a strong, strong feeling that these pure worship songs on the *Throne Room* CD may be the most powerful songs I've ever recorded. Why? Simply because they encourage the believer to bow the knee of the heart and give glory to the God who made them.

Other spiritual songs carry deliverance for different reasons. They may give God glory, for instance, when they sing about what people go through and how God meets them in that certain situation.

But the pure worship songs, the songs that lift up God our Savior for who he is, the songs that sing about the qualities of his character—his holiness, his righteousness, his faithfulness, his goodness—these are the most powerful songs of all! They are the songs that can move mountains in the spirit realm.

1. Hallelujah to the King
(Instrumental introduction)

2. Jesus, You're Beautiful

In that day shall the branch of the LORD
be beautiful and glorious, and the fruit
of the earth shall be excellent and comely
for them that are escaped of Israel.
—Isaiah 4:2 KJV

The very first song on the CD begins with the name of Jesus. That's the way I wanted it to be. To have his name first. I wanted people to know right from the beginning that this CD has no other purpose than to glorify him.

I'll never forget the first time I heard the song "Jesus, You're Beautiful."

I was listening to Sara Groves's CD. Her CD was wonderful, and I'm so grateful that I listened to the whole thing, because if I hadn't I would have missed "Jesus, You're Beautiful." It was the very last song on the album. And when this song began, it just took me right into the Lord's presence, and I began to weep in my bedroom where I was.

It lifted me up and encouraged me to worship him right there. I had this powerful sense of looking on him in my spirit and experiencing the beauty of who he is. And I knew that's what I wanted this CD to do. I wanted it to lead people to him in that way. Because once you're with him and once you see him, how can you help but worship him?

3. THRONE ROOM

And immediately I was in the spirit:
and, behold, a throne was set in heaven,
and one sat on the throne.

—REVELATION 4:2 KJV

I've known Andraé Crouch for years, but this was the first time I ever sat down to write a song with him in person. It was truly a phenomenal experience. If I didn't know God was a just God, I'd be tempted to think that he wasn't when I see the magnitude of talent he has given this man! Really! When you look at the anointed gift this one musician has brought to the body of Christ over all the years, you have to step back and be amazed. He is incredible.

That day we wrote together, Andraé sat down at the piano, and worship songs just poured out of him. I used up so many tissues crying and rejoicing and worshiping and crying. It was hard for me to remember what I was doing there. I just wanted to worship God. I loved so many of Andraé's new songs. But when he started playing "Throne Room," it immediately captivated my heart. I had been asking the Lord for direction on how I was going to shape the CD. At first I didn't exactly know how I would use it. But I knew that I wanted the CD to be about true worship, worship in the highest form. And that's exactly what happens in the Throne Room. So suddenly I knew that God was giving me my answer— the shape of the CD and the title all in one. What a great experience!

Andraé wrote some of the song while we were there. And I took the work tape home and finished writing it. The whole time I was working on it at home, I kept having this unreal feeling. I couldn't believe I was writing a song with Andraé Crouch! I kept thinking, *I hope he likes it!* Even if he hadn't liked what I had done and he had done it all over again, I wouldn't have cared. I knew the song was going to be great in the end. But when Andraé heard what I had written, he said he was truly blessed by it.

To me, the song "Throne Room" creates the setting for intimate worship. I can almost see the scene in my spirit—entering huge doors that open before a throne. We know from the description in Revelation that the Throne Room where we'll worship in the Lord's presence is going to be an incredible place (see Revelation 4:1–4). We can look forward to being there where there is only light. Where there is no darkness at all. Where those who know him will come before him face to face and call him holy. I think this song really creates that image.

Every time I hear "Throne Room" on the CD, I have to smile because I know for sure that it was God's timing, the way it all came together. Andraé is such a busy person, and for everything to fall into place the way it did so he could take the time to meet with me to write—and for him to have exactly the right song with exactly the right theme—I can't help but feel that it was one of those amazing God-ordained things! And I'm so thankful.

I appreciate Andraé Crouch and the way God has used him for years to write so many incredible songs that have been anointed to bring the whole body of Christ together in unity by tearing down racial barriers. I know so many people who would join me in saying thank you to my brother for sharing his gift with the body.

4. HOW GREAT THOU ART

Great is the LORD, and greatly to be praised
in the city of our God, in the
mountain of his holiness.

—PSALM 48:1 KJV

I've always loved the powerful hymn "How Great Thou Art." I can't remember a time when I didn't know it. I knew I would sing it one day on a CD, but until now the time has never been right.

When I decided to do a worship CD, the words of "How Great Thou Art" immediately came into my mind because it's such a natural worship song. It's about God's greatness and his awesomeness and the intimacy of the love I have for him. It catalogues some of the wondrous things he has done and then it says over and over again, "Wow! How great you are, my awesome and amazing God! How great you are!" I love that. It's impossible to focus on those words and keep your heart from worshiping.

That song is as powerful today as it was when it was written many years ago. My prayer is that God will shine a light on that great old hymn for some members of the younger generation who may have lost sight of it, or for those who maybe have never even known it at all. I don't want the kids of today to lose the powerful old music of the church. This is their heritage, and it's so important for them to hang on to it.

You know, there's nothing about being new that makes music great. Music is great in direct proportion to the power it has to connect our heart to God. God anoints certain songs with that kind of power. And "How Great Thou Art" still has that kind of spiritual power. That's why we need to pass it down to our kids. They need what it says and what happens inside of us when we sing it and when we hear it sung. Our kids need that kind of power today.

5. YOU'RE SO HOLY

And the four beasts had each of them six wings

about him; and they were full of eyes within:

and they rest not day and night, saying,

Holy, holy, holy, Lord God Almighty, which was,

and is, and is to come.

—REVELATION 4:8 KJV

I started making up the song "You're So Holy" while doing a live worship

concert a long time ago. The melody just came to me during worship, and

as I would sing a line, the singers would repeat after me. It happened spon-

taneously. While I was singing it in worship that night, I just let it flow with

no real need to put it into any form. But something told me that night

that I would finish it one day, even though I had no idea what I would

use it for at the time.

When I decided to do this CD, I remembered it, and I knew this was

the very spot that this particular song had been waiting for. This was the

perfect fit. And when you hear it on the CD, you know it's right. It's a

song magnifying who the Lord is and saying things you know are being

said in the Throne Room.

Through the years the Lord would bless this little melody anytime I used it in worship. Every time I would sing it, people would begin to worship. So I knew it was a powerful, simple melody, and I knew he was in it. When I got around to completing the song, I wrote the words and the melody. Then my producers, Cedric and Victor Caldwell, added the instrumental arrangement.

6. Oh Thou Most High

I will praise thee, O Lord,

with my whole heart;

I will shew forth all thy marvellous works.

I will be glad and rejoice in thee:

I will sing praise to thy name,

O thou most High.

—Psalm 9:1–2 kjv

I thought I was finished writing for the CD. I actually felt like I had enough songs. And then one day this melody came to me. I had been reflecting on Psalm 9 and the words "Oh Thou Most High" stayed with me. The melody that I got really blessed my spirit.

To me it's a refreshing song. Very light, very airy. It's a song about making a choice. It brings the will into the act of worship. The psalm says I will praise you with all my heart. I will tell of your wonders. I will be glad. I will rejoice. I will sing to your name. I think too often we wait to see how we feel before we decide if we will worship the Lord. The psalmist is saying I will do all of these things. You are my God, so I will myself to worship you. It's my choice, my decision to pour out my love on you, Oh Thou Most High. I choose to bring a sacrifice of praise. Because you are my God, I will sing, I will worship, I will praise you.

Once your will is set in his direction, it becomes one of your favorite things to do. It actually is my favorite thing. I love nothing better than to bring him glory!

7. BY THY BLOOD

And they sang a new song:
"You are worthy to take the scroll
and to open its seals,
because you were slain,
and with your blood you purchased
men for God
from every tribe and language and
people and nation.
You have made them to be a kingdom and
priests to serve our God,
And they will reign on the earth."
Then I looked and heard the voice
of many angels,
numbering thousands upon thousands,
and ten thousand times ten thousand.
They encircled the throne and
the living creatures and the elders." . . .
In a loud voice they sang.

—REVELATION 5:9-12

I was in prayer at our church, "Born Again" Church in Nashville, one morning. We had a powerful time in the Spirit that day, and I remember I got my Bible and it almost automatically fell open to Revelation 5. I read the passage about how Jesus was worthy to take the book and open the seals and how his blood purchased men for God from every tribe and language and nation. I began to sing those words from Revelation. It was such a powerful moment. Then much later during my prayer time at home, I got the chorus to "By Thy Blood." As I sang that chorus to the Lord, I began crying, and I sang it again. Then I had to stop myself in the middle of my worship, as much as I hated to, because the part of me that is a good steward of the songs God gives me was saying, "You'd better get this song down on tape." I could feel that it was going to be a good song. So I did. And then when I played the tape back and listened, the tears came again, because the song reminded me of how real his sacrifice was.

I think a lot of times we let ourselves get out of touch with the reality of the Cross. We say in such an offhanded way, "He died on the cross." We've gotten so used to hearing that phrase that we don't let ourselves feel the horror of what Jesus went through for us. That he came down from glory to this sinful planet because he loved us so much. That he put on human flesh because he cared so much for us. It wasn't just a picture in a frame or a story in a Sunday school lesson. He really did it. He heard the mocking. He felt the shame. He suffered the unbelievable pain of the beating and the cross on his back and the nails in his hands and his feet. And he bled real blood for us.

When we allow ourselves to get in touch with that, our heart has to break. And the tears come. But because of his blood sacrifice we are now part of his royal priesthood. Now we can approach the throne boldly. Now we can fellowship with his Father, because we can come as God's sons and daughters. And we know that our life doesn't have to end in death but it can go on forever with him. This is the glory of the Cross and the blood.

8. HALLELUJAH TO THE KING

Then I heard what sounded like a great multitude,
like the roar of rushing waters and like loud
peals of thunder, shouting: "Hallelujah!
For our Lord God Almighty reigns."

—REVELATION 19:6

This was one of the songs that Andraé Crouch played for me the day that we got together. Andraé writes almost every day, so he probably has hundreds and hundreds of songs in his head that never get to the recorder. Songs are just in him. They flow out of him like water from a fountain. It boggles my mind!

He played me any number of powerful songs, but this one just totally blew me away because it had an almost heavenly quality. That's why we used the instrumental version for an introduction to the CD. The chorus is a sweet melody. And of course, "Hallelujah" is the highest praise.

Like so many of Andraé's songs, I feel that the power of this one is in its purity and simplicity. If you can get into the message of this one and really sing it from your heart, bringing glory to the King of kings, you'll find yourself in his presence.

I heard my son, Alvin, walking through the house the other day singing this song, and it really did my heart good to think that these words had already gotten into that young man's heart. He had only heard it a few times on the new CD and already he was singing it. It had grabbed him. Now I call that an anointed song!

PART TWO:
SONGS OF PRAISE AND ADORATION

These praise songs, unlike the worship songs in Part One, center on thanking and adoring God for meeting the deep need we have for him in our life.

9. THIRST FOR YOU

O God, thou art my God; early will I seek thee:
my soul thirsteth for thee, my flesh
longeth for thee in a dry and thirsty land,
where no water is.

—PSALM 63:1 KJV

Randy Phillips, of Phillips, Craig, and Dean, sent me a tape from his publishing company of "Thirst for You," the first song on the "Praise and Adoration" section of the CD. It was written by John Ragsdale, Jr.

I love Randy's taste in music. I have recorded so many of his songs in the past because over the years I've found that his songs generally touch my heart. I think one reason Randy's writing moves me is that he's a pastor who writes from a pastor's heart. So the emotions he expresses ring true with me. The words are always sensitive and genuine.

This lyric expresses our deep need and our inner thirst for a relationship with the Lord. Nothing else will fill that need. Nothing will satisfy us but Jesus.

To say that we thirst for him is a perfect image. I know without a doubt that my spirit needs the Lord every bit as much as my body needs water. Without water, my body will eventually die. And in the very same way, without the Lord in my life, spiritually I will die. I truly thirst for him. I believe this is why David prayed in Psalm 51:11, "Take not thy holy spirit from me" (KJV). He knew that apart from the Lord he would die. He was thirsting for the Lord.

I wanted this song to be first on the "Praise and Adoration" section of the CD because it represents us pursuing our relationship with the Lord. The Psalmist described the human condition when he wrote, "As the deer pants for streams of water, so my soul . . . thirsts for God, for the living God" (Psalm 42:1–2). There is a deep thirst in every one of us for God, whether we have recognized it yet or not. We were created for him, and nothing else will satisfy that thirst.

So many people are restless, looking here, there, and everywhere for whatever will fill the emptiness in them. We who know the Lord are so blessed because we have discovered the truth that nothing—no amount of money, no amount of fame, no human friendship (however good it may be), no career—absolutely nothing on earth will satisfy the deepest thirst in us. Only Jesus can satisfy that.

10. COME FILL MY HEART

Now the God of hope fill you with all joy and
peace in believing, that ye may abound in hope,
through the power of the Holy Ghost.

—ROMANS 15:13 KJV

I love this song by Bruce Stevens, Tiffany Deonna Martin, and Lanette Crite. I listen to lots of tapes hoping to find songs for my projects, and it's always exciting when I find one that really speaks the deep things of my own heart.

Of course, I came to the conclusion years ago that we are all more alike than we are different. So this song probably speaks the deep prayer of every believer's heart, and that's what makes it a powerful song. It stays very much in the same vein as "Thirst for You," and I like these two songs back to back.

In a way, this is a universal prayer, and a very simple prayer. It asks the Lord to come while I'm waiting—while I'm empty and needy and thirsty—and fill my heart. It's a very vulnerable song. It says to the Lord, "I'm in a place of surrender. I'm waiting on you, Lord. Because I know you can fill me. I know only you can satisfy me. Only you can give me what I need in order to do what I need to do." It's the prayer we pray when we're ready to hand our lives over and get serious with God. I love to be in that place with him. That's where he wants to get us, and it's where we all need to be!

11. MERCY SAID NO (DEDICATED TO RONALD)

Praise be to the God and Father of our
Lord Jesus Christ! In his great mercy he has
given us new birth into a living hope through
the resurrection of Jesus Christ from the dead.

—1 PETER 1:3

Mercy. What a beautiful word! Without the Lord's mercy, none of us would be here.

When I heard this song I knew I just had to record it because it so clearly described the incredible warfare that took place over my brother Ronald's life when his heart ruptured on the operating table. So many people look at things with the carnal mind, but after what we experienced, I'm more aware than ever how real the spirit world is. It's more real than the natural world, even though we can't see it with our eyes.

The testimony of what our family went through is one I'll tell and retell until Jesus returns, because when you see someone you love literally come back from the dead, you know the power of God in an awesome and amazing way. I look back at Ronald's surgery as one of the most terrible and yet one of the most wonderful times of my life. The worst and the best. Because we knew what was happening.

This song says, "Life and death stood face to face. Darkness tried to steal my heart away. But mercy said no." Those were the words that described the battle to me. They just took me back to the hospital chapel where the whole family huddled together in prayer for Ronald.

I remember someone would come in and report to us that he was not doing well. And then that terrible moment when someone came in and said, "They've lost him. He's gone." But we wouldn't let ourselves believe it. I believe mercy was saying to us, "No. Don't you let him go." And so we said, "No. We can't doubt. Ronald needs us to have faith. We've got to fight. We've got to keep believing." That's the way we were talking to each other.

So there in that chapel we laid out on the floor and we cried out— the whole family. And I don't know how long it was, but before we knew it, somebody came in and said, "Ronald's going up to recovery!" And we were all screaming and jumping up and running down the hall.

It seemed to us like the whole hospital was celebrating. There were so many saints in the hospital who had been praying with us, letting us know they were with us. And when the back of that stronghold broke, it seemed like a flood of joy poured over the whole hospital. I'll never forget it!

I guess that's the beauty of the pain we go through. It's in the pain that we understand God's healing. It's in the darkness that we see his brightest light. It's in the lowest times that he comes in and lets us get to know his mercy and what an amazing Savior he truly is!

12. All in Your Name

And whatsoever ye shall ask in my name,
that will I do, that the Father
may be glorified in the Son.
—John 14:13 KJV

My brother Carvin wrote this song, and I just love it. I love the message because I have found that everything I need or want is in the name of Jesus. There are things that I may want that are bad for me, that's true. But when I line my life up with his, there is nothing that I want that lies outside of him and his name and his character. When I'm worshiping him, he's everything to me, so I can ask for anything and it won't be anything that is outside of his will for me. The reason that's true is because all I want is what he wants for me.

A lot of times people, even Christians, forget the power of his name. It's funny how people go to restaurants and use their name to get a good table or use their name to get good tickets or whatever they think they need. And you hear people dropping names in order to impress others: maybe the name of a sports personality or an elected official or a movie star. But in the light of who Jesus is, these people just fade out of sight and their names have no importance.

The name of Jesus is the only name that matters. Jesus is the name that contains everything of value that we will ever need: all authority, all power, all dominion, all knowledge. And only by the name of Jesus can you get to the Father, not by any other name. It is the name that is above every other name. And at the name of Jesus every knee will bow and every tongue will confess that Jesus Christ is Lord to the glory of God the Father (see Philippians 2:9–11).

13. NO ONE ELSE

Remember the former things of old:
for I am God, and there is none else;
I am God, and there is none like me.
—ISAIAH 46:9 KJV

This is a love song that shows the Lord himself as the obvious choice over every other thing or person or relationship on earth. Even the best that this earth has to offer pales in comparison.

Some of the great names of the Lord are brought into this lyric—names like Alpha and Omega, the Beginning and the End, the Lily of the Valley, the Reigning King, our Refuge, our Rock, our Fortress, and our Deliverer. There is no one else who even comes close to Jesus Christ! As much as I love my husband (and I really love my husband!), my marriage relationship doesn't come close to my relationship with the Lord. There's no one else like Jesus. My kids are amazing! The best. They are awesome human beings. But there's no one else like Jesus. He's in a category all by himself.

Sometimes I get to the point where I wonder, "Can I really love you this much, Lord? Can I ever love you like you love me?" And the answer is, "Yes!" Because it's his love that's in me. I can't do it myself. But when I allow him to love through me, I can return to him that same awesome love he gives to me!

What a powerful God he is! He loves us so much that he allows us to return that same powerful love to him.

14. Hallelujah Praise

Let everything that has breath
praise the LORD. Praise the LORD.

—Psalm 150:6

I love to worship God, but I love to praise him, too!

I believe in quiet times with the Lord when I slow down and still my heart and really focus on him. I can't do without those times. But I also love to shout on the mountaintop of praise about who he is! I love to boast in the Lord. That's why I felt that I just had to include a song of celebration. When you think about who he is, your heart can't help but celebrate.

I think about the day that he came down the streets of Jerusalem riding on a donkey, and the people were finally able to see him as a king. They were so excited that they were throwing down palm branches in front of him and crying out, "Hosanna! Blessed is he who comes in the name of the Lord!" (John 12:13). Do you think those people were whispering? I don't think so! I'm pretty sure they were shouting and jumping up and down and totally excited! I believe we've got to have some times when we let the Lord know how excited we are about his love for us. We've got to celebrate who he is and who we are in him. Hallelujah!

15. Just Like You Jesus

Be imitators of God, therefore, as dearly loved
children and live a life of love.

—Ephesians 5:1–2

I was talking to my singers one night just before we were getting ready to go out and minister. We always have a time of self-examination before our ministry time, and we were dwelling on the fact that Jesus is our example. Someone commented that people don't seem to be wearing those little "What Would Jesus Do?" bracelets as much as they used to. Someone else said that maybe it's because people started realizing how hard it is to do what Jesus did.

That really made me start thinking about it.

What did Jesus say when he talked? How did he live and love and act? He was the perfect man. What was it like when he walked on the earth? If we were to keep these things on our mind, would it change the way we walk through our days? In Jesus's life, he was always pleasing the Father. Our life should be lived with the same thought constantly in mind.

Jesus spent a tremendous amount of time in prayer. He had his Father in his thoughts and in his conversation. He only did what the Father told him to do. I believe the Father is also trying to tell us what to do in every situation. It's just that most of the time we're rushing in and doing what we think is the best thing without even listening for the Father's voice. If we were doing it Jesus's way, we'd be listening for the Father's voice before we made one single decision on even the smallest thing.

Jesus was walking in God's timing. He was moving in complete obedience in all things. He was our example of a perfect Son and a True Worshiper.

Can I really live "just like Jesus"? I know that I can't do it by myself. And it's tempting to think that I can't do it at all. But his Word says that I can. And his Word doesn't lie. His Word says, "Be perfect, therefore, as your heavenly Father is perfect" (Matthew 5:48). He wouldn't ask me to do something that is impossible. If he says to do it, then he knows there's a way that I can.

So what is the way? When I surrender and get out of his way and let him take over, he'll change my heart. And that leads us to the next song.

16. A Heart Like Yours

I will give them an undivided heart and put a
new spirit in them; I will remove from them their
heart of stone and give them a heart of flesh.
—Ezekiel 11:19

There's no way we can ever live like Jesus lived unless he gives us a heart like his.

What can we change on our own? We can change our mind and change our hairdo and redecorate our home and get a new wardrobe and a new job. But the Lord is the only one who can change our heart. And we can never live like him unless we have a new heart, a heart like his.

Out of the heart comes everything. Peace and joy and faith and wholeness come from a heart like his. And from the heart come the motives. So often we may find ourselves doing the right things, but then we realize that we're doing them for the wrong reasons. That's when we need to get alone with the Lord and say to him, "Lord, I've got a heart problem here. Please change my heart." And he will.

Sometimes we can even be worshiping with the wrong motives. If our motives are wrong in worship, then everything is wrong. But if we're sensitive to the Lord, he'll reveal those wrong motives to us and help us start worshiping him in Spirit and in truth.

It's God's will that we become true worshipers. And when something is God's will, he will move heaven and earth to help us do that thing. He wants us as close to him as we can possibly be. He longs to open the windows of heaven and pour out more and more of his love on us. Our only job is to surrender to him on a daily basis so that he can daily give us more of himself. But the Lord is such a gentleman, he will never force us to do anything. He leaves the act of surrendering up to us. And that's where it has to start.

I'm praying for you right now that if you haven't found it yet, today will be the day you discover the secret of surrendering, the secret of letting go and letting God be in control. It's really so simple. All God wants us to do is to get out of his way so that he can take over and live his life in us. Most of us have tried doing our life on our own, and if we're honest, we'll admit that we've made a pretty good mess of things more than once. Surrendering can feel pretty great once we make up our mind to do it.

Once we surrender and God totally takes over, we will know that wonderful feeling of "coming home" to our true purpose. All the pieces of our life's puzzle will begin to fit together. And somewhere deep inside of ourselves we will realize that this is where the Lord has been leading us all along. There will be a quiet joy inside, and worship will begin to spring up inside of us so naturally and so beautifully that we will be amazed. Then, in the deep places of our heart, we will understand that this life of true worship is what we were made for. Hallelujah!

A NOTE TO YOU

Dear Reader:

There's no way for me to know where you are in your relationship with the Lord. You may have a strong love relationship with him. You may already live the life of a worshiper. I hope that's true of you! But maybe you have never even trusted Jesus as your Savior. If you haven't, I don't want to end this book without giving you a chance to ask him into your heart. He loves you and wants to direct your life into a path of meaning and wholeness. His arms are always open to those who come to him. If you're ready now, I hope you will pray this prayer.

Your friend,

CeCe

A PRAYER FOR SALVATION

Lord Jesus, I come to you confessing that

I am a sinner in need of a Savior.

Thank you for your promise that if I confess my sins

you will forgive me and give me a clean heart.

(Take time now to confess your sins.)

Thank you for loving me and giving me

this chance to start over with you.

Please come into my heart and live your

life in me. I want to love like you love.

Help me, Lord.

Teach me to worship you.

I pray in your name, Jesus.

Amen.

QUESTIONS FOR REFLECTION

Sometimes I get more out of a book when I take time to pause and reflect on what I've read. These questions from each section of *Throne Room* will give you a chance to go back through and give the book a little thoughtful, prayerful consideration. I've also included some Scripture verses for you to dwell on.

You may want to use these questions: (1) on your own, (2) with a prayer partner, (3) with a prayer study group, (4) with a worship team in your church, or even (5) on a choir retreat. Regardless of how you use them, I believe that prayerfully reflecting on these questions and verses will give the Lord an opportunity to enrich your worship experience.

As you work through the questions, you might want to write out your thoughts, prayers, and ideas in a notebook or a journal.

PART ONE:
WELCOME TO THE WONDER OF WORSHIP

1. Do you find it hard to let go of your own thoughts and shut down your mental distractions in order to focus on the Lord in worship? If so, why is it hard for you?

2. If worship can build faith, kindle joy, transform lives, inspire hope, heal hearts, comfort sorrows, draw us closer to the Lord, and allow us to see him as he is in all his awesomeness, why do you think many people don't worship more than they do?

3. Can you see worship as "a taste of heaven" that we can experience every day that we're on earth? Explain.

All the earth shall worship You
And sing praises to You;
They shall sing praises to Your name.
PSALM 66:4 NKJV

CHAPTER ONE
THE LORD'S LEADING

1. In what ways do you think worship combats the evil times we're living in?

2. How does worshiping make the Lord's Throne Room a part of our day, every day?

3. Should a worship leader make entertainment part of worship? Why or why not? What should be central in worship?

_Jesus answered, "It is written: 'Worship
the Lord your God and serve Him only.'"_
LUKE 4:8

CHAPTER TWO
SUCH AN AMAZING THING

1. How can worship be simple yet truly amazing at the same time?

2. Do you agree that "the key to deepening in the worship life is surrender"? Explain.

3. Have you ever followed this chain of action that leads to obeying God: "Once we surrender to him, we love him; and when we love him, worship will begin to flow out of us, and then we will long to obey him naturally"? Can you see the logic behind that statement? Explain.

4. What is one thing we can do that is always a total blessing to God?

5. When the Lord is so available to us, why do you think that some people seem to settle for a lukewarm prayer life? What can we do to respond more to God's desire to involve our heart in worship?

———

Before me every knee will bow;
by me every tongue will swear.
They will say of me, "In the LORD alone
are righteousness and strength."
ISAIAH 45:23–24

———

CHAPTER THREE
LIVING THE WORSHIP
LIFESTYLE—NOW!

1. Do you have any experience with "the secret place" of quiet and protection where we can approach God as worshipers and know his fellowship?

2. What could Paul teach us about living an overcoming lifestyle?

3. Do you think it is possible for us as Christians to live our lives "before an audience of One"? What benefits would there be to living like that?

_____

In this world you will have trouble.
But take heart! I have overcome the world.
JOHN 16:33

_____

CHAPTER FOUR
WHO BENEFITS FROM WORSHIP?

1. Does the worshiper have to be worshiping to affect a lost world? Think of some ways the Lord can shine through to the lost world in the life of a worshiper.

2. "Being Christ" in a situation might make some people uncomfortable, just as Christ himself made people uncomfortable. Can you think of some examples?

3. What has to happen to "the flesh" before our worship can be a blessing to the Lord?

---

*I have been crucified with Christ and I no longer live,
but Christ lives in me. The life I live in the body,
I live by faith in the Son of God,
who loved me and gave himself for me.*
GALATIANS 2:20

CHAPTER FIVE
A WORSHIPING HEART

1. Why do we need to develop good habits of worship? Shouldn't the life of a worshiper just be totally free and easy? Yes or no?

2. How can "should" and "ought" thoughts turn your precious time with the Lord into a dull obligation? Can you think of any ways to make your worship time more special?

3. Have you ever considered charting out your whole day, beginning by putting the Lord, his Word, and worship at the very center and everything else around him? Are you willing to try it?

4. In what way is each day a "rehearsal for eternity"?

Come, let us bow down in worship, let us
kneel before the LORD our Maker.
PSALM 95:6

CHAPTER SIX
MOVING INTO THE LORD'S PRESENCE

1. Have you ever felt that you have to "polish up your sins" to make them sound less bad than they really are so God won't be shocked or grossed out? God loves nothing better than a child who will "come clean" with him. Read the words of 1 John 1:9 and celebrate the goodness of our God, who loves to forgive us and clean our hearts.

2. Why is surrendering so important in worship? What is your personal definition of spiritual surrender?

3. Although music is not worship itself, music is part of our worship. Explain.

4. Give your own description of worship and what it means to you. Have you deepened in your personal relationship with the Lord through worship? In what ways? Would you like to grow as a worshiper? Have you talked to the Lord about it?

———

You will make known to me the path of life;
In Your presence is fullness of joy;
In Your right hand there are pleasures forever.
PSALM 16:11 NASU

———

CHAPTER SEVEN
WORSHIP AND SPIRITUAL WARFARE

1. What does the following statement mean to you: "The ways of worship are the weapons of our warfare"?

2. Jesus wants you to have a clear identity as his person. What does it mean to "worship your way back into clarity" when you've lost sight of who you are in Christ?

3. Why should you worship the Lord even when things seem to be bad or negative, even if you're hurting?

4. Why should you worship the Lord when you feel wronged by another person or persons?

————

The weapons of our warfare are not carnal,
but mighty through God to the
pulling down of strong holds.
2 CORINTHIANS 10:4 KJV

————

CHAPTER EIGHT
HOW WORSHIP CHANGES THINGS

1. Do you find it possible to worship the Lord through much of the day? At home? In the workplace? In the car? Other? Explain or discuss.

2. Would you be willing to pray this prayer every day: "Lord, this day help me to stay before you in a worshipful attitude of heart. Thank you for being in control"?

3. If you could get "a God's-eye glimpse" of yourself, who do you think you would see? Do you think you have an idea of the purposes the Lord desires for you to walk in? Discuss.

4. As we lift up Jesus in worship, what will he do? (See John 12:32.)

Oh come, let us worship and bow down;
Let us kneel before the LORD our Maker.
For He is our God,
And we are the people of His pasture,
And the sheep of His hand.
PSALM 95:6–7 NKJV

CHAPTER NINE
WORSHIP AS A HERITAGE

1. What has every child created by God inherited as a destiny? What do you think happens in some lives to "derail" that destiny?

2. How do you think the Lord can use you as a worshiper to break any negative strongholds over your family and heal anything that has been wounded? Or how do you think he could use you as a worshiper to multiply faith and spread it to the next generation?

3. Have you felt the Lord stirring up an excitement in you about worship and what it can mean to you and your family? Discuss.

4. How was CeCe influenced by the faith of her parents? How has your parents' faith—or lack of it—influenced yours?

I will sing of the LORD's great love forever;
with my mouth I will make your faithfulness known
through all generations.
PSALM 89:1

Part Two:
Songs on the Throne Room CD

Whether you have worked through these questions for reflection by yourself or in a group, you may now want to listen to the *Throne Room* CD. But I hope you will do more than listen. I hope you will worship along with the singers and the songs.

Preparing your heart in prayer

1) Find a quiet place where you can play the CD. You may be alone or with your prayer partner or your group.

2) Ask the Lord to reveal any area of sin that needs to be confessed. Confess silently to the Lord. (If you are in a group, have each person silently confess to the Lord.)

3) Thank the Lord for this opportunity to come before him and worship him. Ask him to lead you as you seek to draw closer to him in worship.

4) Quiet your heart for a few minutes before beginning the CD.

As you listen, allow the voices on the CD to act as worship leaders.

Feel free to join in the worship with your heart and with your voice.

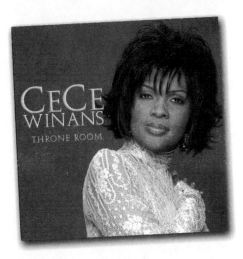

Worship God
by sponsoring a Child.

Yes, I want to sponsor a Child today!

KACWBC

'd like to sponsor a ❑ boy ❑ girl

❑ Please bill me later.

NAME: _____

ADDRESS: _____

CITY/STATE/ZIP: _____

PHONE: (_____)_____ E-Mail _____

❑ Here is my first monthly gift of $26 to help improve the quality of life for my child and their
   entire community

   ❑ Check (payable to World Vision)

   ❑ Bill my monthly sponsorship gift to my credit card:

      ❑ VISA ❑ MasterCard ❑ AMEX ❑ Discover

CARD NO. _____ - _____ - _____ - _____   EXP. DATE: _____ - _____

SIGNATURE (Required): _____

World Vision

Mail today to:

Child Sponsorship
P.O. BOX 688
Fayetteville, GA 30214
1 800 448-6437
www.worldvision.org